THE
INCARNATION
AND THE
CHURCH'S WITNESS

For Shane,

In deep appreciation of
our friendship, admiration
of your scholarship, and
anticipation of many years
of good conversation.

Darrell

Christian Mission and Modern Culture

EDITED BY
ALAN NEELY, H. WAYNE PIPKIN,
AND WILBERT R. SHENK

In the Series:

THE
INCARNATION
AND THE
CHURCH'S WITNESS

D A R R E L L L . G U D E R

TRINITY PRESS
INTERNATIONAL
HARRISBURG, PENNSYLVANIA

Trinity Press International, P.O. Box 1321, Harrisburg, PA 17105

Trinity Press International is a division of the Morehouse Group.

Library of Congress Cataloging-in-Publication Data
Guder, Darrell L., 1939–
    The incarnation and the church's witness / Darrell L. Guder.
      p. cm.
    Includes bibliographical references.
    ISBN 1-56338-310-1 (pbk : alk. paper)
    1. Missions—Theory.   2. Incarnation.
  BV2063 .G875 2000
  266'.001—dc21   99–057256
                                                    CIP

Printed in the United States of America

99 00 01 02 03 04   10 9 8 7 6 5 4 3 2 1

Contents

Preface to the Series

Both Christian mission and modern culture, widely regarded as antagonists, are in crisis. The emergence of the modern mission movement in the early nineteenth century cannot be understood apart from the rise of technocratic society. Now, at the end of the twentieth century, both modern culture and Christian mission face an uncertain future.

One of the developments integral to modernity was the way the role of religion in culture was redefined. Whereas religion had played an authoritative role in the culture of Christendom, modern culture was highly critical of religion and increasingly secular in its assumptions. A sustained effort was made to banish religion to the backwaters of modern culture.

The decade of the 1980s witnessed further momentous developments on the geopolitical front with the collapse of communism. In the aftermath of the breakup of the system of power blocs that dominated international relations for a generation, it is clear that religion has survived even if its institutionalization has undergone deep change and its future forms are unclear. Secularism continues to oppose religion, while technology has emerged as a major source of power and authority in modern culture. Both confront Christian faith with fundamental questions.

The purpose of this series is to probe these developments from a variety of angles with a view to helping the church understand its missional responsibility to a culture in crisis. One important resource is the church's experience of two centuries of cross-cultural mission that has reshaped the church into a global Christian *ecumene.* The focus of our inquiry will be the church in modern culture. The series (1) examines modern/postmodern culture from a missional point of view; (2) develops the theological agenda that the church in modern culture must address in order to recover its own integrity; and (3) tests fresh conceptualizations of the nature and mission of the church as it engages modern culture. In other words, these volumes are intended to be a forum where conventional assumptions can be challenged and alternative formulations explored.

This series is a project authorized by the Institute of Mennonite Studies, research agency of the Associated Mennonite Biblical Seminary, and supported by a generous grant from the Pew Charitable Trusts.

Editorial Committee

ALAN NEELY
H. WAYNE PIPKIN
WILBERT R. SHENK

Introduction:
Understanding Mission "Incarnationally"

In the last few decades, there has been a notable innovation in the language used around the world when talking about mission and evangelism. Possibly first indicated in the missiological writings of John Mackay, we find a growing emphasis upon following the "model" of Jesus in evangelism and mission (Guder 1994: 417–28). Lesslie Newbigin wrote about "mission in Christ's way" in preparation for the 1989 World Conference on Mission and Evangelism in San Antonio (1987).[1] Since then, the terminology has been well established in the ecumenical conversation about mission. It has frequently merged with a parallel emphasis on the incarnation of Jesus Christ as a theological interpretation of the way that mission is to be carried out. In this sense, the term *incarnation* was used by Pope Pius XII as early as 1945 to describe what later missiologists would call the "contextualization" and "inculturation" of the Gospel (Luzbetak 1995:69). Incarnation has also been a particular emphasis of liberation theologies as they have drawn attention to the humanness of Jesus as an essential dimension of his solidarity with the poor and the oppressed (Bosch 1991:512f).

This focus upon the incarnation of Jesus Christ, the Word become flesh, as a way of talking about and understanding mission addresses at least two major and interrelated concerns in the contemporary debate about mission. It responds, first, to the widespread critique of the modern missionary movement which addresses the way that mission has often been done. Many of the missionary methods and strategies have contradicted both the teaching and actions of Jesus as he trained his disciples to continue his ministry. The message may have been the gospel, but the way the message was made known was often not congruent with the gospel. The attempt to interpret mission in terms of the incarnation of Jesus suggests that the earlier European mission strategies should be replaced by a theology and praxis of mission rooted in and defined by the life and ministry of Jesus.

Second, by focusing on the incarnation as testified to in scripture, this approach suggests a biblical basis for mission that addresses its motivation, its content, and its method in direct relationship to the life and ministry of Jesus. The why, what, and how of Christian witness are being explored exegetically in ways that most pioneers of Western mission would not have considered. This is linked with the rigorous rereading of the biblical record in terms of its first-century setting, made possible by the findings of historical, literary, and social approaches to scripture. We find ourselves now able to cut through the centuries of European interpretation and cultural adaptation of the Gospels. We know more about how the early church functioned, and that knowledge is helping us to rediscover the character of early Christian mission. Much of what results from that study can be drawn together in the concept of "incarnational mission."

By incarnational mission I mean the understanding and practice of Christian witness that is rooted in and shaped by the life, ministry, suffering, death, and resurrection of Jesus. The critical question that motivates this study is this: Can and should the unique event of the incarnation of

Jesus that constitutes and defines the message and mission of the church have concrete significance for the way in which the church communicates that message and carries out that mission?

Understanding mission incarnationally, I will suggest, could prove to be a remarkably integrative way to approach the church's missionary vocation. It could counter the typically Western reduction of mission to one of the many programs of the church. It could recast that mission as the definitive calling of the church. It could seek to read the biblical record in its own terms (although there is always debate about what those terms are!) and to address serious problems in Western mission that have surfaced in this century. Thus, the language of incarnational mission could be both constructive with regard to the biblical and theological understanding of message, and polemical with regard to the context and history of mission, especially in the Western tradition.

Just as any theological concept is susceptible to distortion, there are ways of misconstruing the linkage of Christian mission with the incarnation. It is possible to dilute the uniqueness and centrality of the life, death, and resurrection of Jesus Christ when his incarnation becomes a model for Christian behavior. A primarily ethical or moralistic interpretation of the life of Jesus, such as was characteristic of nineteenth-century liberal theology, often downplays or dilutes the event-character of the gospel. But, as I will argue below, it is that event character, the historical "happenedness" of Jesus' life, that both enables and defines Christian witness. As we seek to explore the missional significance of the incarnation, we need to resist every temptation to dilute the centrality of the incarnation event. The risk represented by the concept of incarnational mission is worth taking, I think, especially as we are challenged to develop a viable mission theology for the Western world, which by common consent is now a very challenging mission field.

1

The Word Became Flesh:
The WHAT and HOW of Mission

Mission consists in incarnating Christ in the given time and place, allowing him to be reborn in the given lifeway.

Luzbetak 1995:133

The foundational and formative event of the Christian movement is Jesus Christ as the self-revelation of God. The life, ministry, suffering, death, resurrection, and ascension of Jesus Christ constitute the gospel of God's gracious rule now inaugurated and breaking into human history. The death and resurrection of Jesus Christ have ended the power of sin and death and have opened the possibility of a new creation, a new and eternal life for all humankind. In Jesus Christ the Savior, God has made the promised healing of creation a reality. In Jesus Christ the Lord, God's sovereign love is accomplishing its saving purpose through the witness of the people called to serve and witness to him. It is to the event of Jesus Christ as God's "Word become flesh" that the Christian community is called and empowered to be, to do, and to say its witness.

In his 1932 lecture to the Brandenburg Mission Conference, Karl Barth articulated the essential centrality of God's self-revelation in the incarnation of Jesus Christ as it shapes and defines the church's missional action.

> To be an action of the church means: a certain form of the confession of God's self-revelation in Jesus Christ, a certain form of that particular human action which seeks to be understood as obedience to the call of Jesus Christ as the Lord, an attempt to do his will, that is, to communicate his message, the message about Jesus as Lord, as the creator, reconciler, and redeemer of humanity. That Jesus Christ in truth and reality is this Lord is the content of the Word of God, that is, of that Word which God speaks to humanity and which the church desires to serve in its action (1957: 100f, my translation).[2]

Interpreting mission in terms of the incarnation can be understood as an attempt to define what it means for a very human church to be obedient to the call of Jesus Christ as Lord, to do his will as it communicates his message.

Incarnation is one of the distinctive words in the Christian vocabulary to summarize the gospel event of Jesus Christ. Although the word is not found in the Bible, it is based on John 1:14: "And the Word became flesh and lived among us." With this statement, the evangelist created a powerful picture of God moving into the flesh, *in → carnus*. The thrust of this imagery is missional. It emphasizes that God is active and decisive, that God has taken the initiative in the healing of broken and sinful creation. The scriptures, as Spirit-empowered testimony, witness to God's missionary action, beginning with Abraham and reaching the climax in the incarnation of Jesus, the Son. God the Father has sent Jesus the Son as the Messiah, the Christ, the Anointed One, whose life, death, and resurrection are the epitome and turning point of God's mission to redeem humanity and the world. The Father and the Son send the Holy Spirit to call and to empower the church to carry out its witness to this gracious good news.

With these statements, I have summarized what has come to be known in this century as the *Missio Dei* theology of mission. Indeed, an incarnational understanding of mission can and should be understood as a way of exploring the implications of God's mission accomplished in Jesus for the church's life and practice.[3]

The word *mission* is the Latinized version of the central theme of John's Gospel: *sending*. "As the Father has sent me, so I send you" (John 20:21). As the Father sends the Son, as the Father and the Son send the Spirit, so the triune God sends the church to carry out its mandate of witness. When we use the term *incarnation*, then, we are referring to the specific and historical event in which God's mission reaches its central point and its fullest disclosure. We are also emphasizing the fundamental character of movement and purpose that God's action reveals: "into the flesh" testifies to the fact that God is active and sending within human history. The God of both testaments engages the history of his creation, speaks in such a way that his voice can be heard, and calls people not only to respond to his voice but to become part of his mission. In sending Jesus as the Christ, God draws all of salvation history together, as witnessed to in the Old Testament, and simultaneously opens it up for proclamation to the entire world.

To speak of the incarnation is always to speak of Jesus Christ, the Lord, the once-and-for-all event of God's saving work in the world and for the world. The term *incarnation* includes the whole of that story, as it is described in the Gospels and expounded in the letters of the New Testament. It is a noun that summarizes the "what" of the gospel, rooted in the "why" of God's compassion for creation and purpose to bring about its salvation.

At the same time, it is a concept that, in a very profound way, defines the "how" of gospel witness. There is a fundamental pattern to God's self-disclosure throughout all the scriptures. The way in which God acts is itself an essential dimension of God's mission. We discover what God is like as we experience God's love in action. The what and the how of God's mission, as it unfolds, are congruent and always shaped by the why of God's love. The plot of God's salvation history cannot be reduced merely to propositions about God. Rather, the story reveals both what God intends and how God wants his saving purposes accomplished. One way of talking about this essential coherence and congruence of the message and its communication is to describe God's action as incarnational. By making an adjective out of the noun *incarnation*, we are attempting, theologically, to express this essential congruence of message and its communication of what and how.

At the same time, the emphasis upon the incarnation maintains the profoundly mysterious character of God's action as it continues in and through the empowered witness of the church. It is the Word that was in the beginning, that was with God and that was God, that becomes flesh and graciously enables his creatures to behold his glory, full of grace and truth. That this Word becomes flesh is an event of divine grace. The way that the incarnate Word becomes visible, audible, and knowable in the life, death, and resurrection of Jesus Christ reveals the majestic and sovereign grace of God accomplishing God's purposes within human history. The communication of this good news is now the church's calling: "As my Father has sent me, so I send you" (John 20:21). The only way in which this can happen, however, is through the empowering gift and presence of God's Holy Spirit.

In the earthly ministry of Jesus, the church learns how God's mission is now to be continued after Easter. We learn how our Lord calls and forms his people to be his witnesses. The story of the disciples and of their experience with Jesus on earth is the essential curriculum for the formation of the community that will carry on Jesus' ministry after Easter and Pentecost (I will return to this theme later). It all leads up to the cross and the empty grave. The kingdom that Jesus proclaimed is inaugurated on Easter morning when the power of death is overcome and the life-giving reign of God enters human history in the Risen Lord. Only then does Jesus tell his disciples that they are to be his "sent ones" (see John 20:21; Matt. 28:16ff).

Now, however, when we with the first Christian community look back on the earthly ministry of Jesus, we recognize that from the outset he was calling and preparing those who were to be his witnesses. Mark makes this very plain when he recounts the story of Jesus' calling the twelve. "He went up the mountain and called to him those whom he wanted, and they came to him. And he appointed twelve, *whom he also named apostles*, to be with him, and to be sent out to proclaim the message, and to have authority to cast out demons" (Mark 3:13f–15). At the beginning of the story, when the twelve whom Jesus appointed could understand themselves only as disciples, that is, as students of Jesus, their ultimate purpose was already stated by the Evangelist: they will become apostles, "sent out ones," witnesses to all that God has accomplished in Jesus Christ.

For that to be possible, they must be "with him." They must learn all that he teaches them so that they can proclaim it. They must receive the power that only he can give so that they can challenge the powers of the world in the name of the Sovereign Jesus. As they proclaim the work of salvation accomplished on the cross, they will do it in the way taught them by Jesus as they lived with him and learned by hearing everything he said and watching everything he did. Thus they learned the how of Jesus' mission as they learned the what and the why of the good news.

The emphasis upon incarnational mission is integrative in a very distinctive way. It can help us to keep these two essential dimensions of the gospel story integrated: the salvation event of Jesus' death and resurrection, and his preparation of his missionary people to carry forward into time and around the world the witness to that salvation. It can ensure that the "world" that God loves (John 3:16) will in fact hear the good news about that love.

The continuation of the story in Acts begins with Jesus' final personal encounter with the disciples on the Mount of the Ascension. There the Risen Lord tells the gathered community what their new task will be: "You will receive power when the Holy Spirit has come upon you; and you will be my witnesses in Jerusalem, in all Judea and Samaria, and to the ends of the earth" (Acts 1:8). For the missional theology of Luke-Acts, "witness" is the operative term.[4] It may be seen as the overarching description of the church's missionary vocation. Everything that the Christian community is, does, and says needs to be understood as an expression of its faithful obedience to its Lord and a demonstration of his love for the world. The New Testament literature is, from the first to the last page, a continuing instruction of the church as a mission community so that it can be faithful to its calling. The term *witness* integrates the who, the what and the how of Christian mission. The Christian individual is defined as Christ's witness; the entire community is defined as a witnessing community; its impact upon the world into which it is sent is observable witness; all its activities are, in some way, a form of witness— demonstration of the gracious rule of the Risen Lord. God's Spirit, working in mysterious and gracious ways, empowers this very human and very fallible witness to be the means by which people hear the good news and are invited to become followers of Jesus. The purpose of incarnational witness is "so that grace, as it extends to more and more people, may increase thanksgiving to the glory of God" (2 Cor. 4:15).

The question of the how of mission arises with urgency in the twentieth-century discussion of the church's identity and purpose. I have already alluded to the negative criticism of the Western mission movement that has become commonplace in recent decades. To be sure, this criticism is marked by irresponsible simplifications and generalizations.

But the most devoted supporter of the missionary enterprise must be candid about the many ways in which Western imperialism accompanied Western mission and contributed to the colonialization of much of the non-Western world. The annals of mission history are replete with reports of missionaries whose sacrificial labors truly incarnated God's love in Christ. The leaders of the two-thirds world churches continue to speak with awe and reverence of many of their missionary founders. But the stories are often ambiguous as well. With the best of intentions, Western missionaries went abroad assuming that their task was to take "the gospel of Jesus Christ and the benefits of Western civilization" to the rest of the world. Often they used tactics that could not be justified with reference either to the mission of Jesus or the apostolic church of the first century, as testified to in the New Testament. Although proclaiming the gospel of the incarnate Christ, they continued to assume that modern European Christianity had become the normative shape of God's people for all time. So their evangelistic efforts were often linked with the unquestioned assumption that the churches they founded would end up looking very European.

An incarnational approach to mission also speaks to related problems in the Western churches with regard to their evangelistic work within their own cultures. There has been a growing sense of discomfort with many evangelistic tactics and strategies that have emerged since the onset of the revivals in the seventeenth century. For many today, both Christians and nonbelievers, the term *evangelism* is laden with negative associations. It conjures up pictures of manipulative speakers, simplistic versions of the gospel, false promises of prosperity and happiness, and the exploitive use of clever marketing and communication methods to "bring home converts." At least in North America, the language of incarnational witness appears, as far as I can trace it, to have arisen in reaction to evangelistic tactics that were almost contradictory to the character and actions of Jesus as we experience him in scripture.

An incarnational approach to the how of mission and evangelism also addresses an important scriptural issue. Here we may observe how the constructive and polemic dimensions of incarnational mission interact. It has often been said that the four biblical Gospels are passion narratives with long introductions. Such statements emphasize correctly that the events of Holy Week are the culmination of all salvation history. On the cross, God completed the long-promised work of redemption and overcame every barrier to the reconciliation of his sinful creation to himself.

The criticism can be made, however, that there are ways of emphasizing the work of atonement on Good Friday and Easter that in fact abbreviate the biblical gospel. This happens when the church "skips over" the earthly ministry of Jesus and focuses on the work of salvation. Western Protestantism is particularly prone to do this, but there is a tendency in all Western theology to separate the cross from the earthly ministry of Jesus (over against Eastern Orthodoxy, which emphasizes the incarnation in its own very distinctive ways). The most obvious evidence of this reductionism is the widespread preoccupation with one's individual salvation, effected on the cross, with little attention to the cosmic and communal character of the gospel. As contemporary Western evangelization continues that individualism, leaving out of its gospel proclamation any sense of the comprehensive and radical good news of God's inbreaking kingdom, it reveals that it is just as human-centered as the society it decries.

In summary, the case for an incarnational approach to missional witness is based, on the one hand, on the character of the biblical record; that is, the way in which the church's missionary vocation is shaped by the earthly ministry of Jesus. The emphasis upon the necessary congruence of witness is rooted in God's way of revealing himself supremely and finally in the incarnation of Jesus. The comprehensiveness of the biblical understanding of witness calls for an incarnational interpretation.

On the other hand, this approach helps us to deal with some serious problems in our particular Western context. We see in both our mission history and our current evangelistic practices so much that is contrary to the incarnational character of the gospel. We see a gospel of peace proclaimed in divisive, judgmental ways. We see a Gospel of love conveyed manipulatively, insensitively, condescendingly. We see a gospel of healing obscured by distortions that hurt people and evoke resentment.

Thus we arrive at the concept of incarnational witness as one way of expounding the character of our missionary vocation. In the incarnation of Jesus Christ, God revealed himself as the One who is with and for his creation. Now, as the Risen Lord sends his Spirit to empower the church, we are called to become God's people present in the world, with and for the world, like St. John pointing always to Christ. The most incarnational dimension of our witness is defined by the cross itself, as we experience with Jesus that bearing his cross transforms our suffering into witness.

Incarnational witness is, therefore, a way of describing Christian vocation in terms of Jesus Christ as the messenger, the message, and the model for all who follow after him. To speak of the incarnation missionally is to link who Jesus was, what Jesus did, and how he did it, in one great event that defines all that it means to be Christian. We might put it in terms of the great credal traditions of the church. An incarnational interpretation of Christian witness is an attempt to allow the Second Article, the doctrine of Christ, to define and shape our theology of the Third Article, the Holy Spirit and the church. In what follows, we will explore further the incarnational dimensions of mission.

2

What Incarnational Mission Is and Is Not

―――――――
―――――――

Incarnational witness is focused entirely upon the event of Jesus Christ as God's saving action for all creation.

This is to state the obvious and underline what we have already said. When we speak of the incarnation, we are speaking of the unique event of Jesus Christ, as witnessed to in the scriptures. But the obvious must be stated. That event begins at Christmas and leads all the way to Pentecost. Every chapter in the earthly life and ministry of Jesus is essential to his sending, and to ours. We err if we leap to the events of Holy Week and ignore the earthly ministry of Jesus. We err just as much if we make Jesus into a moral teacher and leave aside the suffering, cross, and resurrection as ancient myths that can no longer speak to "modern humans." Here is where we must tread very carefully when we seek to develop a theology and practice of incarnational mission that is faithful to the gospel and the biblical testimony.

There is a danger, as was said above, in making an adjective out of the noun *incarnation*. This grammatical move can become profoundly reductionistic—and this is frequently happening in the theological discussion today!

11

The use of the term *incarnational* can signal an attempt to drive a wedge between the lifestyle, and especially the teachings of Jesus, and the suffering and death of Jesus as God's atoning actions on our behalf. Not long ago, a church leader in Germany tried to do that very thing by arguing that the church today should focus upon the manger and leave the cross aside. What the world needed today, this leader said, was an emphasis on the happiness and comfort of Christmas, not the pain, suffering, and shame of Good Friday!

Such reductionisms proliferate in twentieth-century Christianity. For instance, there are many ways in which a separation is attempted between creation and the incarnation-atonement event. Creation Theology in this sense can be an attempt to formulate propositions about God's good creation that can be used for ethical or other purposes in total distinction from the atoning work of Christ. This may be done in an attempt to identify a common religious ground with other world religions. It may be done as a way to dilute the scandal of the cross and the particularity of Jesus' story. It may be carried out as an expression of the religious tolerance that has become the hallmark of enlightened Western religion. Often this reductionism articulates, in some way, the conviction that language about God the Creator, that is, First Article theology, is inclusive (especially if one leaves out any reference to "God the Father"). It is capable of embracing many religious points of view. But Second Article language about God the Son, the Redeemer and Savior, Jesus Christ, is considered divisive and offensive. Therefore, we should move away from such a focus, away from the incarnation as a distinctive and unique event, toward a more general and common religious basis.

Sometimes this move to First Article theology is identified with ecological and environmental concerns. The emphasis here might be on the common responsibility of all humanity to be good gardeners of the creation God has entrusted to our care. This approach often claims that Western Christianity must be called to account for being tolerant and even encouraging of the wasting of the environment. For proponents of such a theology, the unique incarnation event is less relevant because it deals with individual sin and one's relationship with God, rather than with our need to be stewards of the world. There is an ironic tension in this move to Creation Theology from Cross Theology, because the exploitation of the environment is precisely an area in which the biblical emphasis upon human sin and the need for redemption should be most obvious!

Another kind of reductionism shifts the accent in the classical Three Articles of the creed in the other direction. Rather than move from the cross to creation, one can move away from the uniqueness of the Incarnate Christ to the Third Article, and talk about religious experience. We find today much talk about spirituality as a general religious phenomenon or given. Religious experience or spirituality can be explored in all its cultural expressions, and certain common themes can be discovered. This then makes it possible to postulate a convergence of religious experience, which functions in turn as a powerful presupposition controlling the whole course of theology. "All the religious roads lead ultimately to the same god." With such an interpretation, one can, perhaps must, ignore or downplay the distinctive centrality of Jesus. He is then *our* way, but no longer *the* way. Such separations, however configured, are always a reductionism of the gospel.

The oldest of these false dichotomies is to divide between the earthly teacher Jesus, emphasizing the moral superiority of his doctrine, and the crucified Savior who is explained away as an invention of Paul or a premodern myth no longer acceptable to enlightened humans. In a variety of ways, one tries to distill ethical injunctions or patterns from the earthly ministry and example of Jesus.

These can be held up for emulation, with reference to the death of Jesus more as a moral model of self-sacrifice for others than the salvific event of atonement. Such approaches obviously represent a very selective reading of the Gospels. They want to deal with Jesus the human teacher, leaving aside his identity as the Son of God, reinterpreting what it means to be Messiah or Christ, and vastly reducing the claim that he is Lord. Rather than "all authority," this Jesus can only claim that "some authority has been given to me in heaven and on earth."

In all of these reductionisms, the adjective *incarnational* can imply that there is something universally valid in the story of the incarnation that can be distilled and made ethically useful without direct reference to Jesus Christ as Savior (the cross) and Lord (Easter and Ascension). The "ethical model" of Jesus, already well known from nineteenth-century liberal theology, continues to haunt much Western Christian conversation. This is all the more surprising in view of the dreadful events of the twentieth century in the so-called Christian West, events that have revealed brutally how inadequate the moral model of Jesus is without the cross that confronts and transforms the sinful human person and the sinful systems of human culture.

The presupposition of such reductionisms is, of course, that the enlightened human person is capable of following the ethical teacher Jesus, if given the proper instruction, conditioning, or therapy. The human problem is not sin, but ignorance, or deficient conditioning (for example, a negative childhood.), or a destructive milieu (all of which are certainly systemic expressions of sin!). There is, in late Western modernity, a continuing resistance to the blunt biblical message of human sinfulness. But if the good news of God's love in Christ is to transform us, God must confront our profound need for transformation and challenge us to repent. The possibility of conversion, as God's continuing work in us, is the core of the good news. It demonstrates the faithfulness of God as the one whose gracious action in Christ can really make us into new people, can initiate a new creation (2 Cor. 5:17). Conversion goes hand in hand with repentance. To claim less for the Gospel of Jesus Christ is to reduce it profoundly.

When we expound both the what and the how of mission incarnationally, we need to be careful always to emphasize that the incarnation is the unique event that founds and forms the church's witness. The event defines how it is to be embodied and thus communicated. That is the real point of making an adjective out of the noun *incarnation*.

Objections to incarnational terminology can also be raised from perspectives very different from the reductionist attempts we have just considered. Karl Barth has called for great caution when speaking of Christian witness as "ongoing incarnation." He raises the point in his analysis of the biblical passages that emphasize "Christ in you" and "you in Christ" (1961: IV, 3, 2d half, p.543). He is concerned that the important theme of the Christian "union with Christ," if it is described as "continuing incarnation," will ultimately distort our exposition of the biblical texts. He is certainly right when we think back to the way medieval Christianity developed its theology and practice of the Lord's Supper. The insistence upon the real presence of Jesus' body and blood as transubstantiated bread and wine, and upon the mass as the reenactment of the unique sacrifice of Christ, was a way of thinking incarnationally that we must reject. It brought the divine mystery and miracle of the once-and-for-all incarnation under the church's control. Barth's warning must be taken seriously.

Yet, it is precisely Karl Barth who develops his entire theology of Christian calling in terms of the prophetic vocation of Jesus Christ. He describes what it means to be Christian precisely in terms of relationship with Jesus, submission to Jesus, formation by Jesus. He expounds the

"distinctive feature of the being of Christians" as "in anal-
ogy to what [Jesus Christ] is." This is very close to what I
am defining as incarnational witness (1961:IV, 3, 2d half,
pp 532ff).[5] Further, he develops his profound theology of
Christian calling as witness within and on the basis of his
monumental Christology, "Jesus Christ, the True Witness."

> The One who has reconciled the world with God in
> himself is not alone as the true witness and proclaimer
> of this event. The world and all its people do not
> encounter him alone. In that they encounter him they
> encounter those (albeit in a very different way, subject
> to and subordinate to his presence and action) whom
> he has called to himself, in the total problematic of
> their humanity, through the Holy Spirit who is the
> power of his word (1959:IV, 3, 2d half, p. 640; my
> translation. See, in the English edition, p. 556).

Our understanding of incarnational witness must
always bear in mind that we live and act as Christ's witnesses "subject to and subordinate to his presence and
action," and that we do so in the "total problematic" of our
own humanity. But the wonder is that Jesus' humanity
reveals what God intends his people to be and to become.
The Christian's life in communion with Christ, which for
Barth forms the very heart of our calling and identity as
witnesses, means that we belong to Jesus, we are constantly confronted and converted by his love, and we discover the very content of our life in serving him.

The emphasis upon the event of Jesus Christ means,
moreover, that incarnational witness, if it is to be faithful,
must attest to the full purpose and scope of God's action in
Jesus Christ. I mentioned briefly the kind of widespread
reductionism that focuses the entire Gospel upon one's
individual salvation. This reductionism goes hand in hand
with a dichotomy endemic to Western Christianity: the separation of personal salvation (one's receiving the benefits of

salvation) from the missional purpose for which we are called and saved. The mission-benefits dichotomy (which I explored in *Be My Witnesses*) is diametrically opposed to incarnational witness.

In the life and activity of the mission community, the fullness of Jesus' good news is to be made known. It is good news about God's love for the world leading to the healing of creation, the establishment of justice, and the overcoming of all systems of oppression that contradict God's rule. Witness to this good news is the church's vocation. That means that the message of God's salvation must always include the call to discipleship leading to apostolate. To experience God's love in Christ is to become a witness to that love not just for oneself but for all the world. To receive the gift of faith, so that we can call God "Abba, Father," and know that we have been restored to fellowship with him, means that we are now to become a part of Christ's body for his service. We can respond to Jesus Christ the Savior only when we submit to him as Jesus Christ the Lord. And all power has been given him in heaven and on earth.

The converse is also true. One cannot be about the work of Christ's kingdom if one does not know Jesus Christ as Savior. There is another form of reductionism found today, especially, in many mainline congregations. People can be committed to the "program of the Gospel" without experiencing the goodness of that news personally. This is often happening when the Kingdom of God is discussed as something we can bring about, rather than our receiving it as God's gracious gift. It becomes then our strategies for justice and our plans for a more equitable society.

The mission-benefits dichotomy is reductionistic in both directions, whether one dwells on the blessings without accepting the call to discipleship and apostolate, or focuses upon the work of the Kingdom without becoming a disciple of Jesus Christ. The personal and the corporate dimensions of the Gospel must be held together!

As we hear the Gospel in the church, we confront our own Christian exclusivism that seeks to hold Christ to ourselves, to have him and his promises for us but not to share them. There is a kind of Dead Sea spirituality in many parts of the church, where the blessings and edification of knowing Jesus are hoarded; it all flows in, but little flows out. There are, especially among conservative, "Bible-believing" Christians, forms of discipleship that are very inward, self-centered, benefit-oriented—in a word, reductionistic.

For Reformed Christians, for example, there is a temptation to read the first question of the Westminster Shorter Catechism reductionistically:

Q. 1. What is the chief end of man?

A.   Man's chief end is to glorify God, and to enjoy him forever (*Book of Confessions* 1994:7.001).

This famous statement is true in that it is God's purpose that all humanity should be reconciled with God in Christ and experience forever the blessings of divine grace and favor. That is, to use the technical term, the eschatological purpose of human existence; this is the goal toward which God's saving activity is moving. Now, however, between Easter and Judgment Day, the chief end of Christian persons is not to hoard the enjoyment of God to oneself, but "to be, to do, and to say witness" to Jesus Christ, so that all people may come to know God and thus glorify and enjoy him forever / (Guder 1983:*passim*). If we read Question 1 restrictively, applying it only to ourselves, then the missionary Gospel requires of us that we repent of that reductionism. We can practice incarnational witness only when we are committed to the service of Christ the Lord who saves us in order to send us.

The Gospel is simple in its clarity but life transforming in its impact. To repent and believe means to turn around and walk in a new direction. It means to receive the gift of new life, life from above (John 3), a new creation (2 Cor.

5:17), a living hope (1 Pet. 1:3). We are called to join the disciples in the school of Jesus and, with them, to be sent by Jesus as his apostolic community to witness to him throughout the world. Our calling is carried out as we "embody," "incarnate" this good news in our forgivenness, our hope, our openness to all people, and our confidence in God's grace.

As a general principle, wherever the particularity of Jesus Christ is avoided or seen as religiously problematic, the likelihood is great that some kind of Gospel reductionism is being espoused. I would insist that such interpretations of the incarnation, with their implications for incarnational mission, miss the mark and must be challenged. We must always return to the point where we began: *Incarnational witness is focused entirely upon the event of Jesus Christ as God's saving action for all creation.*

3

Incarnational Community

_The witness to Jesus Christ is incarnated in the for-
mation of the church as the missional community;
Jesus Christ forms his church for its incarnational
witness by making disciples who become apostles._

The formation of the community of faith is God's strategy
for making good news known to the world. The gospel
event is a story to be told; as it is told and lived out by a
particular people called to be its witness, it continues as
God's saving work within and through human history.
Pentecost is the consequence and implementation of
Easter. What God has done in raising Jesus from the dead,
what has been confirmed in the ascension of Christ, is now
to be made known throughout the world in the witness of
Christ's followers.

It is of the essence of the matter that Jesus was not
concerned to leave as the fruit of this work a precise
verbatim record of everything he said and did, but
that he was concerned to create a community which
would be bound to him in love and obedience, learn
discipleship even in the midst of sin and error, and be
his witnesses among all people (Newbigin 1995:176).

Jesus chose his disciples and prepared them to be the core of the new missionary people whom he would send out as his witnesses. In doing so, he was continuing the salvation story that began with the call of Abraham. Abraham and his descendants were blessed by God so that they, as a people, would be a blessing to the nations (Gen. 12:1–3; 22:15–18; 26:4–5). The selection of twelve disciples to be trained to become apostles (Mark 3:13f) has rightfully been recognized as an intentional linkage with and continuation of the story of Israel. Peter makes the connection emphatically when he describes the Christian community with these terms: "chosen race, a royal priesthood, a holy nation, God's own people" (1 Pet. 2:9). Every one of these words relates back to great themes of the Old Testament; taken together, they effectively summarize the Old Testament vision of the divine purpose for God's people.

The centrality of the community to the gospel means that the message is never disembodied. The word must always become flesh, embodied in the life of the called community. The gospel cannot be captured adequately in propositions, or creeds, or theological systems, as crucial as all of these exercises are. The gospel dwells in and shapes the people who are called to be its witness. The message is inextricably linked with its messengers. If there is good news for the world, then it is demonstrably good in the way that it is lived out by the community called into its service. The early church in Jerusalem lived in such a way that they had "the goodwill of all the people" (Acts 2:47). The lived-out testimony of the Christian community is to become a witness, visible and audible, given in and to the world, so that the gospel will spread.

The objection must immediately come that such an understanding of incarnational witness implies that the church should be a perfect community. There is an ancient understanding of the church as the "prolongation of the incarnation" that moves in such a direction. Such thinking underlies the theology of the church as "the perfect society" as taught by the Roman Catholic Church and is symbolized most obviously in the modern dogma of the infallibility of the pope.[6] This interpretation must be rejected. An incarnational (adjective!) understanding of mission is precisely not a continuation of the once-and-for-all incarnation (noun!), but the continuation of the incarnate Lord's mission as he shaped and formed it. The incarnational witness of the community is not sinless, but rather embodies the reality of grace in its contrition, repentance, and forgiveness. Like the individual Christian, the incarnational community lives and testifies as a people who are *simul justus et peccator* (simultaneously justified and sinners—Martin Luther). What the world should experience in the church is not perfect Christians, but honest Christians whose lives enflesh the real possibility of new life, a new creation, living hope, and confidence that "the one who began a good work among you will bring it to completion by the day of Jesus Christ" (Phil. 1:6). It is essential to define incarnational community very carefully in order not to succumb to the false expectation of ecclesiastical perfectionism. But at the same time, it is essential to hear the repeated emphasis in the New Testament on the character of the church as obedient and faithful witness. Realism about the church's frailty should not result in resignation about the Spirit's power to transform God's people!

The incarnational character of the church is rooted, not in its alleged perfection, but in its submission to Jesus Christ. Its identity is defined by its relationship to Jesus Christ. That is why the followers of Jesus came to be called "Christians" (Acts 11:26), that is, "Christ's persons." This relationship to Jesus Christ is one of response to the One who calls, of submission to the One who commands, of union with the One who gives himself to his own, of dependence upon the grace of the One who equips and forms his people in word and sacrament, and of faithful continuation of his ministry. Every individual Christian, as part of the called people, is thus defined by this shared calling to be Christ's disciples and thus his witnesses. When Jesus calls people to himself, he joins them to his people. The response to that call is, then, always to a relationship of faith in Christ and to his community. This is the primary meaning of baptism.

> The Christian is a person to whom the call to disci-
> pleship has come through the ministry of the disci-
> ples, and who has followed it as the call of the One
> who called, accepted and treated these as His disci-
> ples. If he is in the community, he is a called one. If
> he is not a called one, he is not in the community
> (Barth 1961:IV, 3, 2d half, p. 525).[7]

The church's sense of itself as an incarnational community is focused on its purpose established by its Lord. This obvious statement has many implications for the way that the church has come to understand itself, particularly in the Western tradition. As we struggle today to develop a missional theology for the West, there are two major challenges raised for us by the communal character of incarnational witness.

First, incarnational mission is a challenge to the institutional church of Christendom, in all its forms. If Christ's calling defines the church's purpose, and if the called community is to incarnate the good news, then, to put it bluntly, neither the institution's existence nor its maintenance is to be its priority. The church is not the ultimate and intended outcome of God's grace. Christ did not die only to save Christians, nor to form a church of the saved, but to bring God's healing love to the world. The formation of the church and the salvation of its members are the "first fruits" of God's desire for all creation. Mission, therefore, must not be reduced to institutional preservation, or, in terms of today's crisis of the church in the West, its survival. Its faithful witness takes place as the church submits to Christ's lordship and carries out his work wherever he sends it. The church does not point to itself, but to Christ, following the model of John the Baptist: "He must increase, but I must decrease" (John 3:30).

It is an unavoidable dimension of real historical existence that institutions are formed and continued. The formation of God's people is necessarily an institutional process, both in Israel and in the church. If this were not so, then the calling and sending of God's people would be a docetic, nonhistorical "spiritual" process with little relevance to the world God loves. The problem is not *that* the church is institutional but *how* it is institutional. From the beginning of his ministry, Jesus challenged the institutional forms of God's elect people because, in many ways, they had become a betrayal of God's mission. Whenever we read about the religious leaders of the Jews in the Gospel accounts, we should put ourselves and our church leaders in their place. Jesus' polemic against the religious leaders revealed the great diversity of ways in which the institution then and now can reduce and distort its incarnational mandate. Jesus' message to those who bear responsibility for the "religious establishment" is a constant call to repentance.

The institutional church has a subtle but powerful interest in bringing the gospel under control and making it manageable. This has always been true. As defenders and beneficiaries of the institution, we are challenged by the mandate of incarnational mission to examine how we function critically. The question that the incarnational understanding of mission places before the institutional church is this: Is our communal institutional life an embodiment of the good news? Does the way we live, decide, spend money and make decisions as organizations reveal both the character and purposes of God for humanity?

Second, incarnational mission is a challenge to the individualism that dominates Western culture. If the gospel can be incarnated only in and through a community, then the individual Christian must be defined and understood in terms of his or her membership in that community. The individual Christian is constitutionally dependent: he or she is part of an organic whole that lives and functions only as all its parts exercise their mutual interdependence. This does not discount the distinctive gospel experience of the individual Christian. But that experience is rooted in God's preceding action through the community and must enrich that community. We believe as individuals because God has been at work in the community of faith through the ages to bring the gospel to us and us to the gospel. Further, God's Holy Spirit weaves each individual's faith story into the story and witness of the entire community. In the New Testament, the gospel is addressed to the plural "you," to the community that is called, that has responded, and that continues to be sent as a missionary people. If we are to witness to the gospel incarnationally, then we will take very seriously the way in which we relate as individuals to the corporate church. We will take just as seriously the need to reflect critically and repentantly on the way the institution relates to its members.

How can the church respond to these challenges? How shall the incarnational community be formed in such a way that it does not claim any kind of spiritual perfection for itself, lives in constant submission to its Lord, and radically overcomes individualism by inseparably linking the personal and corporate dimensions of faith? This happens as the community is formed by its Lord. The New Testament Gospels provide that formation. We are called to follow the disciples into their experience with Jesus as their Teacher and Master, in order to carry on their apostolic mission.

In the New Testament world, the disciple was the person who submitted to a teacher in an intimate and comprehensive relationship of learning, imitating, and following. Jesus' disciples, in the typical pattern of rabbinical teaching, left their vocations and normal routines and lived with him. They were disciples as the result of Jesus' action. He called them and invited them to follow him and become fishers of people. They did not apply for the position, but responded to his call. Everything they then experienced with him was essential to their formation. They memorized his teachings, remembered his actions, and accepted his message as the purpose and content of their lives. They were disciples in order to become apostles, students of Jesus in order to become his messengers. Discipleship is not an end in itself, but missional in its orientation: it leads to apostolate, to "sent-outness." "As the Father has sent me, so I send you" (John 20:21).

The basic character of incarnational mission emerges out of this intimate relationship of discipleship. This witness (both the "persons as witnesses" and their "impact as witness"—*martyroi* and *martyria*) is formed by Jesus Christ, whose work through his Spirit is the continuation in the gathered church of what he began with the first community of disciples. This is an essential part of what we mean by the "apostolicity" of the church. The relationship that the first disciples had with Jesus continues in every particular community of faith in its relationship with its Lord. Here is the heart of Christian worship, especially the Eucharist as the concrete experience of Christ's presence, receiving us into his presence in order to send us out as his people. How to do Jesus' mission, then, is learned from Jesus in every generation of the church, through all the ways God's Spirit enables us to hear Christ's word and respond to his call.

That is made emphatically clear at every level of the New Testament witness. The earliest literature, the letters, stresses the reality of the new life that each community is now living out in response to the gospel of Jesus Christ. The epistles were all sent to Christian communities that were already in mission. That is how they understood themselves, as witnesses to the Risen Christ. "In the reporting of

Jesus' final words in the Gospels and Acts we should see
not a command for the early churches to obey but an affir-
mation of what they found themselves doing" (Hunsberger
1994:135).[8] The salvation accomplished by Christ on the
cross now made it possible to live as God's people in an
entirely new way, with new hope and confidence in God,
and with a new purpose as the sent-out community. The
ethics of evangelistic living were taught in the concrete sit-
uations that the epistles addressed. The epistles thus continued Jesus' formation of the mission community, making
disciples into apostles.

The error of understanding incarnational community as
perfected community is clearly rebutted by the New
Testament letters. They were all addressed to particular
congregations in specific contexts. They were grappling
with problems of all kinds in their various settings and
were clearly not perfect communities. Had they been, the
New Testament letters would, for the most part, not have
been necessary. Yet the apostolic authors consistently
address these communities with language that defines their
incarnational character:

"To all God's beloved in Rome..." (Rom. 1:7); "To the
church of God that is in Corinth, to those who are
sanctified in Christ Jesus, called to be saints..." (1
Cor. 1:2); "To the church of God that is in Corinth,
including all the saints throughout Achaia..." (2 Cor.
1:1); "To the saints who are in Ephesus and are faithful in Christ Jesus..." (Eph. 1:1); "To all the saints in
Christ Jesus who are in Philippi, with the bishops
and deacons..." (Phil. 1:1); "To the saints and faithful brothers and sisters in Christ in Colossae..." (Col.
1:1); "To the church of the Thessalonians in God the
Father and the Lord Jesus Christ..." (1 Thess. 1:1);
"To the exiles of the Dispersion in Pontus, Galatia,
Cappadocia, Asia, and Bithynia, who have been chosen

and destined by God the Father and sanctified by the Spirit to be obedient to Jesus Christ and to be sprinkled with his blood…" (1 Pet. 1:1–2).

The constant themes of these salutations are God's action in calling these communities into being through the apostolic witness, their identity as God's chosen people (*ecclesia* = called-out community), and their witness in the particular places where God has placed them and is sending them.

The Gospel accounts, in terms of the timing of their composition, follow and build upon the basic instruction in Christian witness that we find in the epistles. But at the same time, they tell the story of Jesus' discipling of the first apostolic community for the specific purpose of shaping that same process in successive generations of Christians. These scriptures invite all Christians to experience Jesus in the relationship of students following their master, just as did the first disciples as apostles-in-training. We, as Christians who know and submit to Jesus Christ as the Risen Lord, learn from Jesus' earthly ministry how he intends us to make his good news known. We study the Gospels, then, in order to be formed into a missionary community that will continue to incarnate the Gospel.

This means that we learn to read scriptures from the basic assumption that they are intended to equip the community for mission. That is, we learn to read scriptures missionally, guided by the fundamental understandings of a missional hermeneutic. Incarnational witness results from the continuing translation of biblical discipleship into the particular mission fields where we are sent as communities of faith. Wherever the Christian community finds itself, and whatever the particular challenges it faces in its context, its task is always to translate the gospel so that this good news can be heard, seen and responded to. Its witness defines every aspect of its life.

4

The Comprehensive Character of Incarnational Mission

———————

Jesus Christ's discipleship defines every dimension of the Christian's life: incarnational witness is comprehensive.

"His discipleship, which is the history of the relationship of the Christian to Him, embraces the whole life of the Christian." (Barth 1961:IV, 3, 2d half, p. 536). "Witness" as the overarching concept defining Christian vocation points toward the comprehensiveness of incarnational mission. The term describes what it means to be a Christian both corporately and individually. It defines the nature of Christian living as witness: "You will *be* my witnesses" (Acts 1:8). It makes the life of the Christian community come together into a corporate demonstration of the gospel: "By this everyone will know that you are my disciples, if you have love for one another" (John 13:35). It makes every aspect of Christian behavior into an instrument of God's communication: "Conduct yourselves honorably among the Gentiles, so that, though they malign you as evildoers, they may see your honorable deeds and glorify God when he comes to judge" (1 Pet. 2:12). Witness in all its aspects is the constant presentation, through the life of the faith community, of evidence that points people to

31

God and demonstrates the truth of the gospel. It is, as I emphasized in *Be My Witnesses*, the being, the doing, and the saying of the gospel.

The practice of incarnational mission challenges the church today at a number of points where we find ourselves trying to limit the scope of our calling. These are, so to speak, variations and extensions of the reductionisms to which we have already referred. They are constant reminders of our tendency to conform gospel witness to expectations or objections that our world, our context, wants to impose upon the faith.

The world is rarely neutral toward the gospel. Like the evil spirits cast out by Jesus, the powers and principalities of our world recognize that Jesus is a threat (see also the quotation from 1 Peter in the first paragraph!). They may evade his claims by rejecting him; there is constant evidence of that rejection. Their more effective strategy, however, is to enlist the Christian community in various forms of gospel reduction, by subtle or more direct means persuading us that there are good reasons to domesticate the gospel, tame Christ, and make him and his kingdom fit into our patterns and plans. What Satan could not tempt Jesus to do in the desert, the church has constantly done as it has allowed the gospel to be "conformed to this world" (Rom. 12:2).

These reductionisms dilute the incarnational character of mission by dividing what should not be divided and by neglecting or even excluding what should be included in our witness. The thrust of the biblical message is emphatically holistic. The root meaning of salvation is healing, which has to do with making that which is broken whole again. When the gospel is defined in terms of reconciliation, it refers to the way that God through Christ restores divided and broken relationships: the relationship of the creature to the Creator, to other creatures, to oneself, and to the world of created nature. When the gospel is defined in terms of redemption, it refers to the way that God through Christ's death releases sinners from the bondage of sin and sets them into the wholeness of freedom and hope. When the gospel is defined in terms of forgiveness, it refers to God's removal of our guilt and overcoming of our rebellion through Christ's atoning self-sacrifice on the cross. Instead of separation from God, we discover that God has drawn us into a new relationship to himself as his children and thus to his whole creation that he loves.

This wholeness has expanding dimensions that go far beyond the healing of the individual. God's salvation in Christ heals human divisions between races, nations, genders, and social classes. It overcomes the virtually insurmountable barriers between Jews and Samaritans, and even more radically, Jews and Gentiles. It de-centers human centers of power and draws us into new communities of service and mutual submission. It rejects reliance upon violence and redefines human interactions radically as we are empowered to love our enemies. In the eschatological visions of both the Old and New Testaments, the outcome of God's saving work will be the overcoming of all the hostilities that mark creation, joining lions and lambs, infants and asps, and martyrs and persecutors in a new heaven and a new earth. It is not possible to describe the healing and saving purposes of God too comprehensively. Incarnational witness is fundamentally open to the continuing discovery of surprising ways in which God heals what we have long since come to regard as incurably broken.

The most sweeping of the gospel claims is made in the simplest and most concise confession of the New Testament church: Jesus Christ is Lord. As the writer of 1 John presses home, this is the essence of the gospel message. The lordship of Jesus Christ, to whom all authority has been given in heaven and on earth, is a constant challenge to the world's security and vested interests. It is the crucial heart of the church's witness. But it is the most diluted and reduced dimension of our evangelization.[9]

All of these and many more dimensions of God's healing work are essential themes of gospel witness. They are all aspects of the evangel, the gospel, to which we are to witness. But the call to evangelize evokes all kinds of reductionistic responses. The comprehensive character of incarnational witness is frequently betrayed in the ways that we choose to evangelize. We find that, as the church goes about its mission, there is constant division of what is not to be divided and neglect of what must be included.

Evangelization is, at its core, communication. It is making the story known. Its intention is not only to tell the good news, but also to invite those who hear to respond and to become part of the witnessing community. Jesus' earthly ministry is the school of evangelization. We learn from his ministry of proclamation the diversity and creativity of gospel proclamation. It happens in the routine conversations of daily life, in parables, in arguments, in discussions of politics, economics, social conflicts, and in expositions of the biblical tradition. What we learn from Jesus in the Gospels is that the verbal communication of the gospel relates to every aspect of life and society. As the message of God's rule (the Kingdom of God), the evangelistic message both states and demonstrates how all of life is confronted and embraced by God's saving purposes. Jesus teaches us and challenges us to tell the whole story when we communicate the gospel.

The comprehensive character of incarnational evangelization is lost when the gospel we proclaim speaks only to the individual and his or her personal salvation (I spoke to this already in the discussion of the mission-benefits dichotomy, but it is so great an issue that it needs to be repeated). Much American evangelism makes of the gospel a highly individualistic and private affair, protecting the hearer and potential convert from facing the radical claims of Christ's lordship. It is aptly described by Dietrich Bonhoeffer as "cheap grace," when the gospel we offer is